AUB.

ISBN: 978-1-913642-26-6

Book designed by Aaron Kent

Edited by Aaron Kent

Broken Sleep Books (2020), Talgarreg, Wales

Contents

The Men We Are Meant To Love   7
Gwerful Wets Her Petticoat   11
Gwylchu Pais   11
How Gwerful Will Fuck Dafydd Llwyd   12
Gwerful Mechain yn ateb Dafydd Llwyd   12
Gwerful Asks Dafydd Llwyd About a New World   13
Gwerful Mechain yn holi Dafydd Llwyd   13
Gwerful Tells Dafydd Llwyd How She Will Fuck Him   14
Ymddiddan rhwng Dafydd Llwyd a Gwerful Mechain   15
Gwerful Tells Dafydd Llwyd About the End
  of the World   16
Gwerful Mechain yn gofyn i Dafydd Llwyd   16
Gwerful Curses a Man for Beating a Woman   17
I'w gŵr am ei churo   17
Ode to the Cunt   18
Aubade After A French Movie   21
Because This Love   27

Notes on Translations   29
Thanks and Acknowledgements   31

Yng ngoleuni yr ugeinfed ganrif nid yw
Gwerful Mechain namyn putain. (In the light
of the twentieth century, Gwerful Mechain is
nothing more than a whore.)
Leslie Harries, 1933.

I hate men who are afraid of women's
strength… I only believe in intoxication, in
ecstasy, and when ordinary life shackles me, I
escape, one way or another.
Anaïs Nin in her diary, 1933.

Aubade After a French Movie

Zoë Brigley

The Men We Are Meant To Love

we were told about them as girls those men
who would fuck you gently or hard depending
on what you wanted men who never shamed
you for the choices you made when you didn't
know those men going down on you in
the shower one hand on each of your thighs
and a tongue in your vulva men washing
your hair gently with long firm fingers the men
who would spoon you on nights when you slept
with your fear or men who wanted to kiss you
for hours or spend a day on each part of you oh
those men who would cook delicious food that
you would eat in bed before fucking again the men
who sit and listen and say something in return
that cracks open the egg of your knowing
that coaxes out something that you didn't
see a shiny voice that makes you shudder
with the great surprise of it what we wouldn't do
for those men what lengths we would go to what sweet
intimacies we would spread before them what delicious
ways to please we would find for those good men
who feel it too who open up who read books and
share who never spread their legs on the train or
mansplain at meetings men who maybe groan
at housework but do not expect a fanfare when
stacking the dishes or plates do not grow bitter
because they must do what their fathers never
did those men who do not laugh with the boys at
the stolen photo of a naked lover that a friend
flashes on his phone do not shove a woman into
the spare room at the college party do not touch
the behind of their co-worker do not force
their lover to have an abortion do not prevent
their lover from having an abortion do not assume
do not seize do not feel entitled do not do not do not

and you my lover staring into the red distance
are you one of those men
                                            or not?

In touch with the erotic, I become
less willing to accept powerlessness,
or those other supplied states of being
which are not native to me, such as
resignation, despair, self-effacement,
depression, self-denial.

Audre Lorde, 'The Uses
of the Erotic,' 1978.

Translations After Gwerful Mechain

fl. 1460-1502

Gwerful Wets Her Petticoat

In my camisole wet through—my chemise
            and my sweet, silk panties too,
        I'll never be dry again, unless it is true
        that good fucks pass by like rainclouds in June.

‡ ‡ ‡

Gwylchu Pais

Fy mhais a wlychais yn wlych—a'm crys
            A'm cwrsi sidangrych;
        Odid Gŵyl Ddeiniol foelfrych
        Na hin Sain Silin yn sych.

How Gwerful Will Fuck Dafydd Llwyd

Lit thighs open to punish your moans—I swear
                    I'll fuck the length of you on and on,
       as your balls ache and rub upon
       the down between my legs where we join.

‡ ‡ ‡

Gwerful Mechain yn ateb Dafydd Llwyd

Cei bydew blew cyd boed blin—ei addo
                Lle gwedde dy bidin;
       Ti a gei gadair i'th eirin,
       A hwde o doi hyd y din.

Gwerful Asks Dafydd Llwyd About a New World

Always the everyday emptiness—to watch
and lose a wilderness.
Has the time come as we undress
for a world to arrive that is not this?

‡ ‡ ‡

Gwerful Mechain yn holi Dafydd Llwyd

Pa hyd o benyd beunydd—yn gwylio
Yn gweled byd dilwydd.
A pha amser, ddiofer Dafydd.
Y daw y byd ai na bydd?

Gwerful Tells Dafydd Llwyd How She Will Fuck Him

Your penis means pleasure—hard, lengthening
                 to a bell's clapper, loud my cries
          when it's cuffed inside, clasped by sighs:
          sunk to the hilt & fucking like fire.

All cunt and hungry to exhaust you—my darling,
               to lull your cock where it grew;
          your balls rub on the join of us two,
          all of me longing for all of you.

I'm still coming, carrying my love—Cariad;
             what I see is enough
          for you to be my bae. Hot as fuck,
          the delicious length, deep the touch.

Fuck money. Far better the head—of your penis
             enter my pretty body. The bed
          that falters beneath your thrust. How good
          the match struck as ecstasy explodes.

Ymddiddan rhwng Dafydd Llwyd a Gwerful Mechain

Braisg yw dy gastr, bras gadarn—dyfiad
        Fal tafod cloch Badarn;
    Brusner cont, bras yn y carn,
    Brasach no membr isarn.

Hwde bydew blew, hyd baud blin—Ddafydd,
        I ddofi dy bidin;
    Hwde gadair i'th eirin,
    Hwde o doi hyd y din.

Haf atad, gariad geirwir—y macwy,
        Dirmycer ni welir.
    Dof yn d'ôl oni'm delir,
    Y gwas dewr hael â'r gastr hir.

Gorau, naw gorau, nog arian—gwynion
        Gynio bun ireiddlan;
    A gorau'n fyw gyrru'n fuan
    O'r taro, cyn twitsio'r tân.

Gwerful Tells Dafydd Llwyd About the End of the World

Before the wars, we'll look to the stars—more miracles
         happen on oceans than at altars,
      and though presidents do give orders,
      witches strip and dance on the shore.

‡ ‡ ‡

Gwerful Mechain yn gofyn i Dafydd Llwyd

Cyn y dêl rhyfel daw rhyfeddod—ar y môr,
         Mawr yw gwyrthiau'r Drindod,
      A'r prif ar naw'n profi'r nod
      Gwae ynys y gwiddanod.

Gwerful Curses a Man for Beating a Woman

In his chest, let a sharp stone slide—slanted
                down to split his sternum wide:
        kneecaps shatter as hands cry
        to hold the heft of spurting heart inside.

‡ ‡ ‡

I'w gŵr am ei churo

Dager drwy goler dy galon—ar osgo
                I asgwrn dy ddwyfron;
        Dy lin a dyr, dy law'n don,
        A'th gleddau i'th goluddion.

Ode to the Cunt

Every dumb-as-fuck, wasted poet,
all of them mansplainers—
they'll spare me & my sisters if they
know what's good for them—
every one writes empty tweets
for the girls on Wind Street,
long threads, though they take
the best for granted, ffs.
They praise a girl's hair, stitch
her dress with love, her body,
& all around. They praise
the brows over her eyes,
or the lovely shape of her:
how smooth her breasts are:
how arms in bright sleeves
are beautiful, not to mention
her hands. Still, a poet is spelling
his song to the night, thanking
fuck for creating this woman.
No praise though for between
the legs: the space inside
where sperm meets egg,
or the warm cunt: a circle
broken, incandescent, when
I loved—hot as fuck—
the cunt under my skirt.

Fierce cunt: deeper cave: strong
& exact as a walled garden: red
as kite feathers. Beautiful cunt:
opening like a valley: mouth
of two broad lips to suck a spoon,
a finger, or whatever length
she so desires. Cunt swelling
between cheeks behind, I sing
you, red twin. But some men,
virtue-signaling, these "nice"
guys if they have the chance
never fail, the fuckers, to have
a feel, take the space as their own.
So fuck all the witless men,
himpathy poets, & sing
a song to the cunt for riches
no doubt. Queen of odes: silken:
written along two seams: the flag
of a sweet, fleek cunt flutters
a greeting: sharp thicket soaked
with love: a forest proud with
fucking: perfect as it is: tender
border: fur for a fuckable ballsack:
girl's dense grove: deluxe
booty call, or gorgeous bush.
Thank fuck for it.

Sexuality reaches into something very beautiful. It's the duty of a filmmaker to show that this is not impure or ugly. Only artists can see that pornography is only a commercial invention of sex.
                    Catherine Breillat, 2008.

Aubade After A French Movie

Tomorrow's film will be an act of love.
Francois Truffaut

That night if you'd wanted,
she would have let you
fuck her. You knocked
into each other
quite unexpectedly & something
cracked
open, set free
after that. *Dear troublemaker,* she writes,

if you were here with me, I'd
run my lips over
each part of you, kiss
every inch. Remember
the French film, La Fille Sur Le Pont, *where the lovers*
are separated but go on
talking in their heads? If I feel close,
it's because I am, but under a black veil.

So much that is erotic
about lace... so much that is
intimate about stone. How clever
sculptors are, revealing in marble nudes
what we are not allowed
to see as we go about
our days. A veil can both
hide & reveal

a woman's sex, might suggest
what we usually
cover. She woke before anyone else
that morning & sat
in the garden
with the shriek
of blue jays. Yesterday
was a blue bridge, a river & you

walking towards her & how shy
she was when the breeze rushed

under the velvet of her skirt, across her thighs, desire
carried like a sharp
intake of breath. Then there was no peace
without your body
across hers, no peace at all
unless you lay over & under

& with her. Being
completely honest
was both the easiest & hardest
thing in the world & you gave her
such feelings. Here
it begins: with Eros as trouble but
still it draws you. When
you wanted to take her,

to carry her away, she didn't
struggle. She stayed
quite still with her arms around you as
you travelled away into the night. But can
she trust herself? She is piecing herself
together from snatches
of films she's seen. In dreams, she will dance
like Emmanuelle Béart in *Manon des Sources*

naked in the water, knowing herself &
nothing
is wrong. As Béart/Manon,
she will know what kind
of woman she wants to be: a woman about
to combust. Or she will conjure *Amelie,*
herself as Audrey Tatou when Amelie/Audrey's body folds
to water, splashes

in a puddle on the floor. Even
the most cynical
are touched by it—they just
won't admit it. Above her
the moon pulls with heightened
sensitivity & longing. You begin
entering her dreams when
she is near water: swimming

or in the bath, wading in lakes
or rivers & she will have no peace
unless she undresses
before you, unless
you undress before her. Too restless
to sleep or eat, shivering
in your bed. Years ago,
she could bring herself right

to the point of orgasm just
by thinking or
imagining, or she would come
in her sleep, unusual
for women. *Is it like that
for everyone?* she asks you. *So much
out of the brain?* She looks
in the mirror at

her pretty body, the sweet,
little breasts. The last time
she heard that song, she
was naked
in your bed & when
it was over you sweetly
fucked her
—*c'est vraiment dégueulasse*—

& she loved you
in spite of what others
might say. *Il me dit
des mots d'amour… des mots
de tous les jours.* But it's no good
saying it over and again, when
she finds herself running
a corridor in *La Belle et La Bête*,

her cloak fogging
movements, hands grasping,
mistrust flaming the candlewax
so it falls on you
painfully. She sees the mistake
far too late, but now
she is cast out
naked on the grass in the morning light.

Criticizing and suppressing women who harness their sexuality and discuss it in frank — even vulgar — terms is part of a long history of policing women's sexuality.

Brittney McNamara, 2020, on the reaction to Cardi B's '"WAP"

Because This Love

In lips she is sweet; life is in her mouth.
Hymn to Ishtar, 1600 BC

because this love is strong as a rope;
because words on a page are not kisses on the mouth;
because I am strong & I am not strong;

because there is a crack in the eggshell;
because something is tapping its way out;

because I climb to hang from you;
because my body ornaments yours;

because I dreamed in the little hollow;
because you stood over me;
because you unwrapped me;
because my skin was grey & silver under the moonlight;

because I talk too much;
because I say too much;
because there are times when you say too little;

because there is a space behind text where emotion should be;
because I cannot tell what feeling lies behind these letters;

because I pour myself out;
because nothing is left;
because it seems unlikely that I would be that lucky;

because I fly like a goose feather on the wind;
because I cross oceans carried like a seed pod;
because I am the wind itself that blows across the flat land;

because I am visiting you now while you sleep;
because I came out of the water naked to find you;
because I watched over your bedside;
because I left wet footprints on the floor;

because I am looking for you behind my black lace;
because I have given you my body to look at;
because the body is bathed in salt & white fire;

because I am not here, but away in the greenwood;
because you were delivered to me on a hot day in July;
because it was a circling swallow that told me;

because the Lady Ishtar wishes it;
because Our Lady of Paradoxes forces me to bend;
because I am bleeding for you each day;

because you are close, perhaps in the next room;
because I carry your voice inside like my own voice;
because I am as tender for you as I'd be for my own child;

because I dress in blue & look down at the ground;
because I am innocent, but I am not a virgin;
because they tell me that whores are holy;
because I can help what I am no more than a willow can;

because I spend too long predicting what you must think;
because I have laid my armor down;
because I put my armor back on;
because the armor is off again, silver in the grass;

because I took off my clothes in the light of the camera;
because I stood in the window of the studio naked;
because I looked out through the glass with no fear;

because, in mirrors, I could be a cloud or a succulent;
because sometimes in mirrors, I see a woman;
because I laid the length of my body along the studio floor;
because I wore only tulip petals veined with yellow;

because I am soft & smooth & blank as the page;
because I am stripping myself of my skin;
because I am the one who will write myself;
because we could not give each other what we promised.

This love will be the death of me, but now I know
that it will be a good death: one without too much
pain, the pinch when it enters. I still hope for resurrection.

Notes on Translations

This chapbook is dedicated to the Medieval poet Gwerful Mechain (1460-1502) and it includes translations of her poems from Cymraeg (Welsh). I hope to give life to her voice again in these translations, and, through an act of summoning, she might speak through my own poems too to address the present day.

Witty, celebratory, outrageous, and shameless, Gwerful was also extremely skilled at writing in poetic forms of Cymraeg: the englyn, the cywydd, and cynghanedd. Past translations of Gwerful tend to be strict in replicating the original rhyming and formal patterns of the englyn, but the priority of these new versions is capturing the spirit of what is said, seen through a modern lens of #metoo, "slut shaming", feminism, as well as violence against women and against groups with fewer privileges. I do take liberties with the original, because my project is imagining what Gwerful would say in a modern context. Still where possible and appropriate, the englyn's rhymes or half rhymes and cynghanedd-like chiming are employed.

Gwerful is probably best known for her erotic poetry. Gwerful's 'Cywydd y cedor' or 'Ode to the Cunt' still feels fresh and funny today. Praising the vulva, the vagina, or any part of a woman's genitals is extremely empowering in a world of body shaming and labiaplasty. Gwerful is also a very early example of a poet writing about intimate partner violence in the englyn translated here which curses a man for beating his wife. Gwerful's poems do sometimes point to inequalities and abuses, but most of all they represent shameless laughter, and exhilarating joy.

Thanks and Acknowledgements

'Ode to the Cunt,' 'Gwerful Curses a Man for Beating a Woman', 'Gwerful Wets Her Petticoat' and 'Gwerful Tells Dafydd Llwyd About the End of the World' appeared in *Modern Poetry in Translation.*

These translations owe inspiration to Katie Gramich and Jon Stone, especially Katie Gramich whose versions of Gwerful's poems are fundamental and inspirational. Without Katie Gramich's essential scholarly work on Gwerful Mechain, this book would not have been written (see *The Works of Gwerful Mechain,* ed. & trans. Gramich, Broadview, 2018). Also, thanks to these poet/editors: to Fleming Meeks for helping me unearth Gwerful's spirit, and to Kristian Evans for his invaluable advice on Welsh forms and for editing this manuscript.

This chapbook is also dedicated to all the students in my Sexuality Studies classes. How different it would be if we were taught to treat sex ethically, thoughtfully, erotically: to treat it as one of the most beautiful forms of pleasure that human beings can make with each other.

TAENA D'ANESMWYTHYD